HITLER:
THE HOFFMANN PHOTOGRAPHS

VOLUME I

NORTHSTAR'S WWII SERIES
Edited by
Ray R. Cowdery

Translated by
Josephine van Nierop

Cataloging in Publication Data
Cowdery, Ray R., 1941 -
    Hitler: The Hoffmann Photographs, Volume I
    1. History; WWII, Germany
    2. Photography
ISBN Number 0-910667-07-1
First Edition
Printed in U.S.A.
© Copyright 1990 by Ray R. Cowdery

Published by
USM, Inc.
P.O. Box 810
Lakeville, MN 55044-0810
USA

EDITOR'S PREFACE

For years I have guided tours to Europe to "the Ruins of the Reich". These tours were a spontaneous outgrowth of our general interest WWII history and battlefield tours which I guided for thousands of Americans. The interest in Hitler and the German Third Reich is enormous and crosses all lines of politics, religion and society. I have had tour passengers as young as 15 and as old as 80. I've taken hundreds of veterans, students, professors, Christians, Jews and atheists. I have spent countless days and weeks attempting to identify the source of their interest in these times, events and personalities.

The interest, it seems to me, is clear. Well over half the people on earth have been born *since* WWII. The era has predictably passed from the stage of one accompanied by the tremendous horror of war to one largely of historic significance. Observing the people I have guided to the massive killing ground of the Hürtgen Forest, I can detect no more emotion than I can see on the faces of visitors at Gettysburg Battlefield. I do detect precisely the same interest in what happened, how it happened, what equipment was used, how the participants were dressed and why the victory went the way it did.

In this respect, Heinrich Hoffmann has left an enormously valuable and interesting resource in the 2½ million photographs he and his photographers took before and during the Third Reich period in Europe. While one person may look at a photo of Hitler driving through Austria after the Anschluss in 1938 and see Hitler, others will see the Cathedral at Melk while others will see only the Mercedes-Benz car in which Hitler traveled. Many of the buildings wrecked by the war in Europe were rebuilt with the aid of Hoffmann photos.

There is much to be gained and nothing to be lost in a careful examination of all aspects of any conflict, including WWII. The Hoffmann photos in this book will tell us much about the well-oiled Nazi political machine that dominated all of Europe for years. The posture and the expressions on the faces of the subjects in Heinrich Hoffmann photographs tell us more than any text could about their attitude and the degree of their success or failure.

Ray Cowdery
Lakeville, Minnesota USA
1990

NOTE: The Hoffmann photographs and negatives were seized by the United States Army at the end of WWII and are part of the permanent collections of the USA National Archive in Washington, D.C.

INTRODUCTION

The series of photos and books which Heinrich Hoffmann produced as Hitler's official photographer made him wealthy and the most sought after German photographer of the Third Reich period. The Hoffmann books from which this volume was produced are now rare collectors items selling for hundreds of dollars per copy.

Heinrich Hoffmann really was a very fine photographer. His ability and his Nazi conviction came to Hitler's attention as early as 1919. The two became good friends and Hitler passed a lot of time in the Hoffmann studio at Nr. 50 Schellingstrasse in central München. It was there that Hitler met and courted his future wife, Eva Braun, Hoffmann's assistant.

Heinrich Hoffmann was born 12 September 1885 in the city of Fürth, just outside of Nürnberg. He was trained in photography by his father and uncle who were both well known photographers in the highest circles of German royal society. He worked for Hugo Thiele, the court photographer of the Grand Duke of Hessen in Darmstadt, for Langbein in Heidelberg and Theobald in Frankfurt. Moving to London he published art books in addition to his work as a photographer.

In 1910 Hoffmann returned to Germany and opened his own studio in München. He was very successful, and during WWI served as a photographer in the Bavarian Army. In 1919 he published his first photo book in Germany; the same year he met Hitler. Hoffmann joined the Nazi Party in 1920, was quickly admitted to the inner circle and became a confidant of Adolf Hitler.

Upon Hitler's release from prison in 1924 Hoffmann became his personal photographer. He alone was franchised to make and sell pictures of the Fuhrer. By 1929 Hoffmann had opened branches in Berlin, Vienna, Frankfurt, Paris, The Hague and had hired a new assistant that was to effect his future dramatically - Eva Anna Paula Braun, the 17 year old daughter of a München schoolteacher.

When Hitler succeeded to the office of Reichschancellor in January, 1933, Hoffmann's fortunes took another positive turn. He published his most successful book, *Hitler, wie ihn Keiner Kennt (The Hitler Nobody Knows)* which made him very wealthy. It was followed over the next few years by other similar books including this one.

Hoffmann was a close friend of Wilhelm Ohnesorge who became Minister of Post for the Third Reich. With his knowledge of photographic and book royalties, Hoffman and Ohnesorge combined to establish the system by which Hitler was paid a royalty for each time his likeness was used on a German postage stamp.

Hoffmann's daughter, Henny, married the Hitler Youth leader Baldur von Schirach which further served to weave the family into the fabric of upper-class Nazi society.

In 1938, Hitler appointed Hoffmann Professor out of respect for his craft and his artistic sense. It was Hoffmann who pre-selected works of art which were to be displayed at the annual exhibitions in the House of German Art in München. In 1940, Hoffmann was elected to the Reichstag from the district of Düsseldorf-East.

Heinrich Hoffmann was incarcerated at the end of WWII and tried as a Nazi profiteer in 1947. The court sentenced him to 10 years in prison (which was later reduced to 3 years, then increased to 5 years) and confiscated most of his personal fortune. Hoffmann died in München on 16 December, 1957.

The photos in this book are taken from the book *Hitler Erobert das Deutschen Herz (Hitler Wins the German Heart)* published by Zeitgeschichte-Verlag in Berlin in 1938. That book was a composite of three earlier books, *Hitler in seiner Heimat (Hitler in His Homeland)*, *Hitler Baut Gross-deutschland (Hitler Builds Greater Germany)* and *Hitler Befreit Sudetenland (Hitler Liberates Sudetenland)*. The H in a wreath on the title page was the logo of the Hoffmann Studio.

THE LIBERATOR

This photo was taken during the night of 13 March 1938 on the balcony of the city hall in Linz.

DER BEFREIER

Aufgenommen in der Nacht zum 13. März 1938 auf dem Balkon des Rathauses in Linz

9

Departure from Berlin
Abflug von Berlin

With
Mit Generaloberst Keitel

In the airplane studying the map of Austria.
Im Flugzeug über der Karte von Österreich

Am Morgen des 13. März / **Kiefersfelden**
The morning of 13 March - Kiefersfelden.

The barricades come down.
Die Schranken fallen

Kufstein

Gebirgstruppen auf dem Marsch
Mountain troops on the march.

Going over the Inn river.
Übergang über den Inn

Einzug in Kufstein
Entering Kufstein.

At the Brenner pass.
Am Brenner

Begeisterte Menschen auf der Salzachbrücke
Enthusiastic citizens on the Salzach bridge.

Salzburg

German Police on the border.

Deutsche Polizeitruppen an der Grenze

The General Staff leaving Muhldorf on the Inn.

Abfahrt vom Generalstab in Mühldorf am Inn

Hitler's entry into the city of his birth, Braunau.

Hitlers Einzug in seine Geburtsstadt Braunau

The border between Germany and Austria ceases to exist.

Die Grenze zwischen dem Reich und Österreich ist gefallen

On the Inn bridge at Braunau.

Auf der Innbrücke bei Braunau

Braunau

22

The greeting for the liberator.
Der Gruß an den Befreier

The Fuhrer passes his birth house in Braunau.
Der Führer passiert sein Geburtshaus in Braunau

Am Abend des 12. März
The evening of 12 March.

Die Geburtsstunde des
großdeutschen Reiches
in Linz

The hour of birth of the
Greater German Reich in Linz.

The people of Linz celebrate their liberator.

Die Linzer Heimat feiert den Befreier

The Fuhrer after many years in the city of his youth.
Der Führer nach vielen Jahren an der Stätte seiner Jugend

At the grave of his parents.

Am Grabe der Eltern

The house of his parents in Leonding near Linz.
Vor dem Elternhaus in Leonding bei Linz

Sein alter Lehrer
His old teacher.

In Leonding

Linzer Hitlerjugend grüßt den Führer
The Hitler Youth of Linz greet the Fuhrer.

With his old Alustrian party-comrades.

Unter alten österreichischen Parteigenossen

Auf der Fahrt nach Wien, vorbei an den Kolonnen der Wehrmacht
Passing a column of troops on the way to Vienna.

A chance meeting on a country highway.
Begegnung auf der Landstraße

31

Underway.
Unterwegs

32

An outpouring of love and jubilation.
Eine Welle von Liebe und Jubel

The Fuhrer greets a marching column outside Melk.
Der Führer grüßt die marschierenden Kolonnen vor Melk

An Austrian honor guard greets their new leader entering the town of Melk.

Eine österreichische Ehrenkompanie grüßt ihren neuen Obersten Befehlshaber beim Einzug in Melk

This is how Melk welcomes the establishment of Greater Germany.

So grüßt die Stadt Melk den Begründer Großdeutschlands

Noon rest in St. Polten.
Mittagsrast in St. Pölten

On 14 March, only 8 days after the Schuschnigg treason, loyalty oaths

Schon am 14. März, noch nicht 8 Tage nach Schuschniggs Verrat, stieg der Treueid

of the Austrian Army to the Fuhrer's Greater Germany rose to heaven.

der österreichischen Wehrmacht auf den Führer Großdeutschlands zum Himmel

Auf dem Wege nach Wien
On the way to Vienna.

A stop in the worker's neighborhood in Western Vienna.

Ankunft in den Arbeitervierteln im Westen Wiens

This is how the Fuhrer . . .
So wurde der Führer

was received in Vienna.
in Wien empfangen

On the balcony of the Imperial Hotel.

Auf dem Balkon des Hotel Imperial

43

The Fuhrer proclaims the new mission of German-Austria to the jubilation

Am Heldenplatz in Wien proklamiert der Führer unter dem Jubel

of the hundreds of thousands gathered on Hero Square in Vienna.
der Hunderttausend die neue Mission der deutschen Ostmark

Arrival of the Fuhrer at Hero Square.
Ankunft des Führers auf dem Heldenplatz

Auf dem Weg zum Ehrenmal
Going to the Memorial

While the liberated Viennese cheer the Fuhrer leaves Hero Square.
Unter tosenden Heilrufen der befreiten Wiener verläßt der Führer den Platz

Die große Wehrmachtsparade vor dem Führer am 14. März
The huge military parade for the Fuhrer on 14 March.

Right from the Fuhrer . . .

Rechts vom Führer Generaloberst Keitel, Reichsführer der SS Himmler, Generaloberst von Brauchitsch, Generaloberst Milch, General Krauß und Reichsstatthalter Dr. Seyß-Inquart

A scene Vienna has not witnessed since its glory days!

Ein Bild, wie es Wien seit seinen Glanztagen nicht mehr sah!

49

German tanks . . . .
Deutsche Panzerwagen . . .

... and field guns roll over the Ring Street!
.. und Feldgeschütze rollen über den Ring!

An unforgettable day: jubilant crowds and shiny weaponry.

Ein unvergeßlicher Tag: Jubelndes Volk und schimmernde Wehr

Österreichische Reiter und Infanterie vor dem Führer
Austrian cavalry and infantry pass the Fuhrer.

Leaving Vienna.

Abflug von Wien

Hitler returns to the capital of the movement after 4 days absence.

Nach vier Tagen zurück in die Hauptstadt der Bewegung

Back in Berlin, Goring greets the Fuhrer.

Wieder in der Reichshauptstadt . . . wo Generalfeldmarschall Göring den Führer begrüßt

Youth welcomes the Fuhrer.
Ein Willkommen dem Führer der Jugend

58   Two million jubilant Berliners . . . .
Zwei Millionen jubelnder Berliner . . .

treat him to a reception never before seen in Berlin.

... bereiteten dem Führer einen Empfang, wie ihn die Reichshauptstadt noch niemals sah

The people of Berlin crowded together on the Wilhelmplatz like never before.

Auf dem Wilhelmplatz drängte sich das Volk von Berlin in Massen wie noch nie

Time and again the Fuhrer thanks his happy people.
Immer wieder dankte der Führer seinem glücklichen Volk

Within 8 days of his departure from Berlin
Nach noch nicht acht Tagen seit seinem Abflug von Berlin . . .

the foundation of Greater Germany was announced by the Führer in the Reichstag.

... machte der Führer dem Reichstag die Vollzugsmeldung von der Errichtung Großdeutschlands

Hermann Göring dankt im Namen des Reichstages und des Deutschen Volkes dem Führer

In the name of the Reichstag and the German people Hermann Goring thanks the Fuhrer.

DANK DER NATION AN DEN BEFREIER

„Sie aber, mein Führer, zogen als Befreier in Ihre Heimat. Sie wurden ihr Befreier, wie Sie uns allen Retter in tiefster Not geworden sind. Sie brachten Ihre Heimat zurück zum Reich als Land mit herrlichen Menschen und reichen Schätzen . . .

Kein Schuß ist gefallen. Kein Rachetribunal hat Bluturteile gefällt. Güte und Verzeihung für die Vergangenheit, Hoffnung und unerschütterliches Vertrauen für die Zukunft; das haben Sie Ihrer Heimat gebracht! Nicht Wunden geschlagen, aber unendlich viele Wunden geheilt. Das war Ihr Werk schon in wenigen Tagen . . ."

Thanks of the Nation to the Liberator

You, my Fuhrer, moved into your homeland as a liberator. You became their liberator, like you became a liberator to all of us in our deepest need. You brought your homeland back to the German Reich, a country with wonderful people and rich treasures. . . .

No shots were fired. Angry tribunals didn't have to pronounce any bloody sentences. Kindness and pardon for the past; hope and complete trust in the future; that's what you brought your homeland!

No new wounds were made, but countless wounds were healed. That happened after only a few days of your work. . . .

(From the speech of the President of the Reichstag, Fieldmarshall Goring, 18 March, 1938)

The Fuhrer conquered on a larger scale than ever expected.

Weit über jedes Maß hat der Führer gesiegt

Im Nordosten des Reiches, in der alten Krönungsstadt Königsberg, gab der Führer am 26. März die erste Parole zur „Heiligen Wahl" am 10. April

On the 26th of March the Fuhrer announced the first slogan for the "Holy choice" in the northeast of the Reich, in the corona-

tion city of Konigsberg, to take place on 10 April.

"I am in the midst of my people" said the Fuhrer in his Konigsberg speech on 26 March, 1938.

„Ich stehe mitten unter meinem Volk!" (Der Führer in seiner Rede in Königsberg am 26. März 1938) 67

"We want to see our Fuhrer" called the hundreds of thousands at the Exhibition center in Leipzig.

„Wir wollen unseren Führer sehen!" So riefen Hunderttausende in der Reichsmessestadt Leipzig

From the Sportstadium of the German capital (still familiar to him
from the struggle period) the Fuhrer spoke to his
Berlin citizens.

**In der aus der Kampfzeit bekannten und vertrauten Kampfstätte des Sportpalastes der Reichshauptstadt
sprach der Führer zu seinen Berlinern**

Sinnbild Großdeutschlands: Linzer Truppen vor ihrem obersten Befehlshaber in Berlin
Symbol of Greater Germany: troops from Linz march in front of their chief in Berlin.

The Fuhrer in Hamburg....
Der Führer in Hamburg ...

.... and in the old Hanseatic city of Cologne.
... und in der alten Hansestadt Köln

"God created us not so we would fade away, but rather so that we can maintain ourselves!"
„Gott hat uns geschaffen, nicht, daß wir vergehen, sondern daß wir uns erhalten!"
(Der Führer in Köln am 30. März 1938)

Dr. Schmidt, the mayor of Cologne, presents the Fuhrer with the salute of the Rheinland in the time-honored Gurzenich.

Der Kölner Oberbürgermeister Dr. Schmidt entbietet im altehrwürdigen Gürzenich dem Führer den Gruß des Rheinlandes

On the Romerberg in Frankfurt aM, hundreds of thousands cheer the Fuhrer with great enthusiasm

In Frankfurt am Main rufen Hunderttausende am Römerberg begeistert nach dem Führer . . .

.... so he has to show himself over and over from the balcony of the Romer.

.... der sich immer wieder auf dem Balkon des Römers zeigen muß

„Das Werk, für das vor 90 Jahren unsere Vorfahren kämpften und bluteten, kann nunmehr als vollbracht angesehen werden. Ich bin dabei der Überzeugung und der felsenfesten Zuversicht, daß dieses Werk, das neue großdeutsche Reich, für alle Zukunft bestehen wird, denn es ist getragen vom deutschen Volke selbst und begründet auf die unvergängliche Sehnsucht des deutschen Volkes nach einem Reich!"

(Der Führer in Frankfurt/Main am 31. März 1938)

The work, that our ancestors struggled and bled for, for 90 years, can be considered completed. I am convinced and have unshakeable confidence that this work, the new German Reich, has future for everybody, as it is carried by the German people themselves and was founded with the everlasting desire of the German people for their own Reich!

Effervescent salute of the Opel-Works in Russelsheim.

Brausender Heilruf der Opel-Gefolgschaft in Rüsselsheim

In Stuttgart the Wurtembergers are jubilant for the Fuhrer.

Die Württemberger jubeln in Stuttgart dem Führer zu

A surge of enthusiasm in the city of the "Foreign-Germans".
Wogen der Begeisterung in der Stadt der Auslandsdeutschen

"I have performed my duty, 75 million people wanted it".

„Ich habe die Tat vollzogen. 75 Millionen haben es gewollt!" (Der Führer in München am 2. April 1938)

Nightly loyalty oath of the Bavarians on the Theresienwiese in Munchen.

Nächtlicher Treueschwur der Bayern auf der Theresienwiese in der Hauptstadt der Bewegung

An jedem Haltepunkt das gleiche Erlebnis
At every stop the same experience.

A gift for life - an autograph of the Fuhrer.
Geschenk fürs Leben: Ein Autogramm des Führers

No other statesman travels like this. Only the Fuhrer of Greater Germany travels this way: Everywhere along the way
So reist kein Staatsmann der Welt, so reist nur Großdeutschlands Führer: Überall an den Strecken grüßend Volk . . .
greeting the people. . .

. . . workers make sure the road is clear.
. . . Arbeiter sorgen für freie Fahrt

Wo immer im befreiten Österreich der Zug des Führers hält, jubeln Tausende: Ein Volk, ein Reich, ein Führer!

Everywhere his train stops in Austria the jubilant thousands shout: "One people, one Reich, one Fuhrer."

Ankunft des Führers in Graz
Arrival of the Fuhrer in Graz.

A dream come true for the people of Styria: Adolf-Hitler Day in Graz.
Traumerfüllung der Steiermärker: Adolf-Hitler-Tag in Graz

For everybody a good word, for everybody a loving handshake; this is how the Fuhrer greets the victims

Für jeden ein gütiges Wort, für jeden einen lieben Händedruck: So grüßt der Führer die Opfer des Schuschnigg-Systems

of the Schuschnigg system.

The Fuhrer gives comfort and hope to the widows and orphans of the fighters murdered by the Schuschnigg hangmen.

Witwen und Waisen von Schuschnigg-Henkern ermordeter Kämpfer gibt der Führer Trost und Hoffnung   **89**

True helpers of the Fuhrer (left to right):

Treue Helfer des Führers (von links nach rechts): Reichsstatthalter Dr. Seyß-Inquart und Reichskommissar Gauleiter Bürckel

Austrian Hitler Youth and League of German Girls members in front of the Fuhrer.
Leidgestählte österreichische HJ. und BdM. vor dem Führer

Klagenfurt girls - lucky guests of the Fuhrer.

Klagenfurter Mädels — glückliche Gäste des Führers

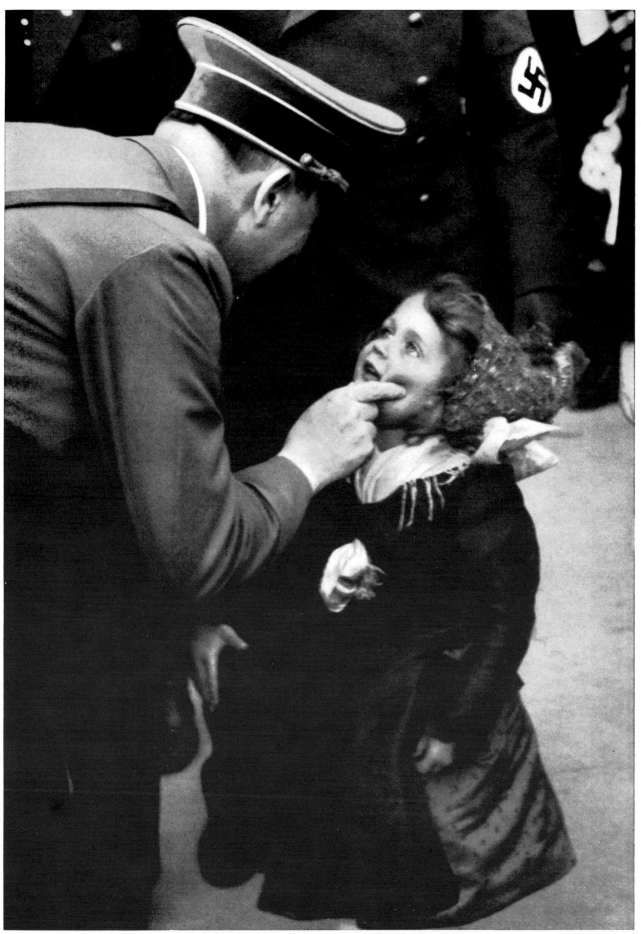

Bright children's eyes are sun rays for the Fuhrer.
Leuchtende Kinderaugen sind Sonnenstrahlen für den Führer

Den Führer sehen und hören . . .
Seeing and hearing the Fuhrer.

The Fuhrer comes. .
Der Führer kommt: . . .

Devoted and solemn at the same time.
... ist Andacht und Weihestunde zugleich

Karnten is his with heart and hand.
... Kärnten ist sein mit Herz und Hand

Entering Klagenfurt.
Einzug in Klagenfurt

A jubilant symphony in the capital of Karnten.

Jubelsymphonie der Hauptstadt Kärntens

All Austria echos again...

Ganz Österreich hallt wider...

. . . from unspeakable happiness.
. . von namenlosem Glück

A heartwarming scene in Villach: moved by inner emotions they stand in front of the Fuhrer...

Herzergreifende Szene in Villach: Erschüttert von innerem Glück stehen sie vor dem Führer ..

... and bring him the salute of the faithful land of Karnten.

... und bringen ihm den Gruß des treuen Kärntnerlandes

Believing. . . Trusting. . . Loyal. . .
Glaube . . . Vertrauen . . . Treue . . .

Gratitude from the Fuhrer - a reward for fighters freed from prison.
Der Dank des Führers — der Lohn des aus dem Kerker befreiten Kämpfers

Arrival in Innsbruck; Tirolian Landesschutzen greet their liberator.
Ankunft in Innsbruck; Tiroler Landesschützen grüßen ihren Befreier

As early as 1920 Salzburg had voted nearly 100% for Germany. At last it can celebrate the fulfillment of its longing.

Schon im Jahre 1920 hatte Salzburg fast 100 % für Deutschland gestimmt, nun feiert es die Erfüllung seiner Sehnsucht

Somewhat different than Schuschnigg thought it would be: the land of Andreas Hofer and bacon makers happily
declares itself to Greater Germany.

Anders, als es sich Schuschnigg dachte:
Freudig bekennt sich das Land Andreas Hofers und Speckbachers zu Großdeutschland

The Fuhrer enters beautiful Salzburg.
Einzug des Führers im herrlichen Salzburg

Der Anschluß bringt Arbeit und Brot: Der Führer selbst beginnt das Werk
The annexation brings work and bread: the Fuhrer himself began the work.

At the start of construction of the Salzburg-Vienna freeway: the Fuhrer hears the pledges of the workers.
Beim Baubeginn der Reichsautobahn Salzburg—Wien: Der Führer hört das Gelöbnis der Arbeiter

A flower-greeting in Tirol.
Blumengruß in Tirol

The creator of Greater Germany in his homeland; a triumphal drive through Linz.
Der Schöpfer Großdeutschlands in der Heimat, Triumphfahrt durch Linz

Jubilant final accord in German-Vienna. In front of the Burg Theater

Jauchzender Schlußakkord im deutschen Wien. Vorbei am Burgtheater ...

. . . the Fuhrer drives to City Hall.
. . fährt der Führer zum Rathaus

The mayor of Vienna requests of the Fuhrer: "Germany, take us in your holy heart!"

Der Wiener Bürgermeister bittet den Führer: „Deutschland, nimm uns an dein heiliges Herz!"

Day of the Greater German Reich.
Tag des Großdeutschen Reiches

The touching and emotional end of the rally in Vienna: Let us pray. .

Der ergreifende Abschluß der Kundgebung in Wien: Wir treten zum Beten ...

The voice of the Fuhrer - the voice of the people. More than 99% of the population vote with the Fuhrer for Greater Germany.

Die Stimme des Führers — die Stimme des Volkes. Mit dem Führer stimmten über 99 % für Großdeutschland

Election-night in the Reichschancellery: The Fuhrer listens to the results of the balloting for Greater Germany.

Wahlnacht in der Reichskanzlei: Der Führer hört das Ergebnis der Volksabstimmung für Großdeutschland

Konrad Henlein at the Obersalzberg.

Konrad Henlein am Obersalzberg

2. 9. 38. Konrad Henlein erstattet am Obersalzberg dem Führer Bericht über die Lage
Konrad Henlein delivers a message about the situation to the Fuhrer at the Obersalzberg.

First meeting of the Fuhrer with Neville Chamberlain.
15. 9. 38. Erste Begegnung des Führers mit Neville Chamberlain

Chamberlain wird am Obersalzberg vom Führer und General Keitel empfangen
Chamberlain is received at the Obersalzberg by the Fuhrer and General Keitel.

Before the meeting at the Obersalzberg.
Vor der Sitzung am Obersalzberg

Chamberlain   Henderson

121

22. 9. 38   Godesberg. Über der Karte der Tschechei
                 Looking over the map of Czechoslovakia.

Chamberlain und Hitler in Godesberg

Von Haus und Hof vertrieben . . .
Banished from house and farm. .

... flüchten 250 000 Sudetendeutsche ins Reich
... 250,000 Sudeten Germans fled into the Reich.

126

Sportspalace Berlin. The Fuhrer starts his historic speech.

26. 9. 38.   Sportpalast Berlin. Der Führer beginnt seine historische Rede

Kufstein. Two statesmen greet each other.

29. 9. 38.   Kufstein. Zwei Staatsmänner und Freunde begrüßen sich   127

128

Aboard the special train from Kufstein to Munchen.

29. 9. 38.   Im Sonderzug von Kufstein nach München

29. 9. 38.   München, Marienplatz

29. 9. 38.   11¹⁰. Ankunft des französischen Ministerpräsidenten Daladier in München-Oberwiesenfeld
The arrival of French Prime Minister Daladier in Munchen-Oberwiesenfeld.

29. 9. 38.   11⁵⁵. Chamberlain wird vom Außenminister Ribbentrop vom Flugplatz Oberwiesenfeld abgeholt
Chamberlain was taken from Oberwiesenfeld Airport by Foreign Minister v. Ribbentrop.

Der Führerbau in München und ...
The Fuhrer building in Munchen.

The working office of the Fuhrer in which the negotiations took place.
das Arbeitszimmer des Führers, in welchem die Verhandlung stattfand.

First meeting of French Prime Minister Daladier with the Fuhrer in the Fuhrer building in Munchen.

Erste Begegnung des französischen Ministerpräsidenten Daladier mit dem Führer im Führerbau zu München

Mussolini and Daladier greet each other in the Fuhrer building. (Behind Daladier
is Leg. Rat Schmidt who was interpreter during the nego tiations).

Mussolini und Daladier begrüßen sich im Führerbau. (Hinter Daladier Leg.-Rat Schmidt, der
in den Verhandlungen Dolmetscher war.)

29. 9. 38.   12⁴⁵. Während der Verhandlungen ...
             During the negotiations.

und in der Pause
and during the break.

in Munchen,

in München

zum 30. September 1938

-30 September, 1938.

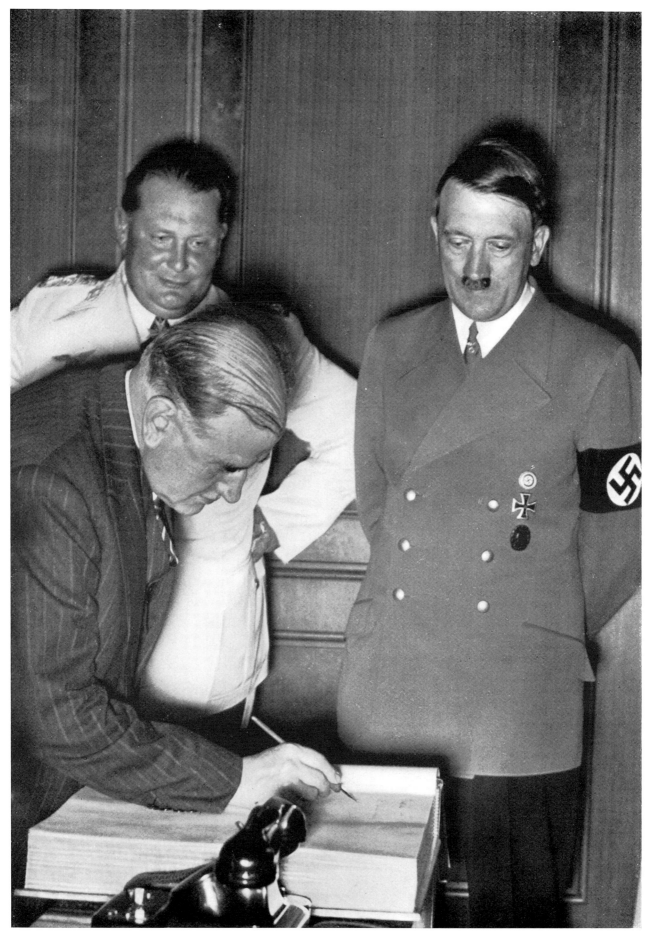

At the Fuhrer's request, Daladier signs the guestbook.

Daladier trägt sich auf Wunsch des Führers in das Gästebuch ein

After the signing of the agreement.
Nach der Unterzeichnung

At the home of the Fuhrer: "never again war between Germany and England".
In der Wohnung des Führers: „Nie mehr Krieg zwischen Deutschland und England"

Der Einmarsch der Befreier
The entry of the liberators.

Jubel um den Führer
Jubilation for the Fuhrer.

So hauste die tschechische Soldateska
Havoc left behind by the Czech soldiers.

Die Grenzen fallen!
The borders come down.

The memorable 1 October, 1938.
Der denkwürdige 1. Oktober 1938

144

The Fuhrer on Sudeten German soil.
Der Führer auf sudetendeutschem Boden

Artillery and armored troops on the march.

Artillerie und Panzertruppen auf dem Marsch

146

Blut kommt zu Blut trotz Not und Tod

The welcome greetings for the liberators.

Der Willkommensgruß für die Befreier

Der Führer ist da
The Fuhrer is here!

Der Führer vor Männern des Freikorps
The Fuhrer with men of the Freikorps.

Wir danken unserm Führer
We thank our Fuhrer.

Flowers for our soldiers.
Blumen für unsere Soldaten

150

The Fuhrer signs in the guestbook of the old-Reich city of Eger.

Der Führer trägt sich in das Buch der alten Reichsstadt Eger ein

Hail Victory on the market square of Eger.

Sieg Heil... auf dem Marktplatz von Eger

Der Führer und Konrad Henlein

Eger, vor dem zerstörten Hotel Victoria, dem Sitz der Hauptstelle der SdP.
In Eger, in front of the destroyed Hotel Victoria, office of the SdP Party.

Bei den Heilquellen von Franzensbad
At the mineral springs of Franzenbad.

Entry in Karlsbad.
Einzug in Karlsbad

Glaube und Erfüllung
Belief and fulfillmlent.

They have to see the Fuhrer.
Sie müssen den Führer sehen

The Fuhrer speaks in liberated Sudetenland.

Der Führer spricht im befreiten Sudetenland

158   A sea of joy.
        Ein Meer der Freude

Der Führer mit Generalfeldmarschall Göring, Konrad Henlein und General Rundstedt
The Fuhrer with

Der Führer und sein getreuer Paladin freuen sich...
The Fuhrer and his faithful Knight-Errant are happy...

Der Führer besichtigt tschechische Befestigungsanlagen   The Fuhrer inspects Czech fortifications.

Tschechischer Bunker mit Laufgraben   Czech bunker with trenches.

Unterwegs   Underway.

Hier sollten Tausende sterben　　　Thousands were supposed to die here.

　　Beim Studieren der Anlagen　　　Studying the construction.

Gefallene Zwingburgen   Destroyed pillboxes.

Der Führer unter seinen Soldaten   The Fuhrer among his soldiers.   163

Gesprengte Straßensperre   Blown up barricades.

Paradeaufstellung der Wehrmacht   The Army on parade.

Der Führer an der Schöber-Linie   The Führer at the Schober-Line.

Der Gruß der Herzen   Greetings from the heart.

The Fuhrer greets the deputy of the SdP

Der Führer begrüßt Amtswalter der SdP.

Der Führer tröstet   The Fuhrer consoles.

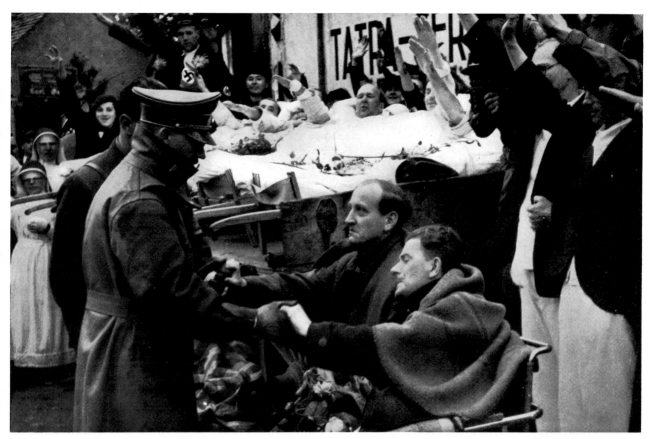

Des Führers Dank — der schönste Lohn!   Thanks from the Fuhrer - the nicest reward!

Der schönste Tag des Lebens...   The nicest day of life...

Heimgeholt und geborgen...   Homelike and secure...

Nach der Befreiung . . .

After the liberation.

Tears of happiness.

Tränen der Freude

Und alle Hungrigen betreut die NSV.! And all the hungry people trust in the NSV!